CW01315565

ALCHEMY
In the Dark

Lola Lawrence

Poetry and prose

Alchemy In The Dark Copyright © 2022 by Lola Lawrence All rights reserved. No part of this publication may be reproduced, distributed, or transmitted in any form or by any means, including photocopying, recording, or other electronic or mechanical methods, without the prior written permission of the publisher, except in the case of brief quotations embodied in critical reviews and certain other noncommercial uses permitted by copyright law.

ISBN: 9798351156255

DEDICATION

*"I remember that time you told me
You said, "Love is touching souls"
Surely you touched mine
'Cause part of you pours out of me
In these lines from time to time"
"A Case of you" - Joni Mitchell*

*T.L.D.
My love, my heart, my muse.
There are no words to express how much
of an influence you've been in my writing, in my life.
So I will simply end with,
I more than love you.*

ACKNOWLEDGEMENTS

Writing has shown a light on who is really in my corner. It also has brought amazing people into my life.

Stephanie, you have become my rock, my creative sister. You challenge me, you create with me. You are irreplaceable.

Jay Willowbay, my editor and friend, your support and creative energy have meant so much to me.

My AJ. Your love and encouragement spur me on. Your invaluable friendship means so much to me. You've been my ride or die for almost 3 decades. You are my best friend and my family. I love you.

PREFACE

Why did I choose "Alchemy" for the title? Alchemy is about transformation. This collection is just that. Writing has helped me heal. Each part of this collection was a profound part in me expressing vulnerability. Learning lessons.

I lived the better part of a decade completely lost. Lost in being something to everyone. Wife, Mother, daughter, friend and a professional. I existed. There was no passion, no lust for life. I jokingly refer to this as my "Frumpy Era." Even my pen my lay silent for fifteen years.

And suddenly one decision set me upon a path that would bring me back to myself. It has brought me passion. it has brought me pain. It has brought me love. Most importantly, it brought me healing. I was thrown into a journey of self-discovery. I was fortunate to meet someone who supported that journey and together through the love we shared, I was able to face my shadows head on. This does not mean it was all rainbows and sunshine. There was pain there too. There was also incredible passion. Love, pain and lust were the alchemical magic behind my transformation.

In this collection there is sweetness. There is darkness. There is lust. And sometimes all three in one moment. Pain taught me lessons. Love gave me strength. Lust gave a passion for life again.

CONTENTS

KISSING SHADOWS 1

BEAUTIFUL SURRENDER 65

IGNITE MY WILD 129

KISSING SHADOWS

Alchemy in the Dark

The Dark Parts

Pain has a purpose. It tells us what is wrong. Pain teaches lessons. It lets us hear our dark side, our shadow side. The alchemy of pain can be profound. I've spent the better part of my life hiding from it. Vulnerability was weakness and I wanted to keep it at bay. The Universe, the divine, whatever you choose to call it had other plans. This section is me allowing myself to feel the pain and transmute it into something beautiful.

Alchemy in the Dark
♥

Do not awaken her heart
Nor entice her wild to play
If you have no intention of staying

Alchemy in the Dark

I've tried to forget you
But I have magnets in my blood
For your bones

Alchemy in the Dark
♥

Madness lost and heaven bound
to flirt with the line
between passion and utter insanity
burst forth into vivid adventures
blurring the lines
languish in the veil between the worlds
because the alternative
is sipping stagnant water
on dull shores with grayscale monotony for company
feet barely touching shallow edges
and wondering how I'm still drowning

Alchemy in the Dark

Vulnerability used to be such a dirty word. I feared it. I hated it. Vulnerable meant weak and I prided myself on being the strong one. The stable one. The warrior and protector. I could take on the trouble of the world and fix the pain of others. I welcomed the vulnerability of others. Almost craved it. While my love and compassion of others is/was genuine, it was also my escape. Burying myself in others meant I didn't have to acknowledge my own pain. Writing gave me a place to scream.

Alchemy in the Dark
♥

if you could feel the way I love you
see yourself through the lens
you'd never allow tainted fingers
to claw your soul ever again.

Alchemy in the Dark

♥

obliterate the sentinels
Iron shackles on burning skin
self-imposed prison I've forgotten how to live
your scream of freedom
caught now in my lungs
slay my chains
captive to the fear
to the shadows of doubt
this love my talisman against myself
bind to you forever
making sense of me
your heart calling my name
reckless but sure
surrender to the fallout
break me down
until its only your voice inside my head

Alchemy in the Dark

With you I'm so safe
so completely myself
it scares me
Aching to be touched
awed by the provocative benevolence of your skin
like with the most gentle collision
of fingertips upon my cheek
and the carefully erected parchment walls
surrounding my bones will simply disintegrate
collapsing in prismatic destruction
caught off guard in love
leaving me vulnerable to a kill shot

Alchemy in the Dark

dead air fills the space
where laughter used to live
devoid of the excitement
you once held for me
despondent voice creates the rift
fading in slow waves
distance tastes bitter
I swallow the panic
Dubious the prattle in my mind
maybe the picture is mistaken
designed by doubt
feeding lingering irrational fear.

Alchemy in the Dark

♥

Fingers interlaced
under shadowed moons
fervent whispers
in the tone of dreams
lit up a gray sky
like casting diamond runes
your mouth brimming
with adventure stories
not yet written
kiss our way
across the world
satin midnights
in idyllic towns
bodies in scandalous display
where glistening sweat
lends its shine to shy stars
every tale exploded on my skin
Gasping in delicate webs
slyly beguiled
your romancer's tongue
busy spinning plush yarns
and I so naively enthralled
didn't realize
the wool was moth eaten

Alchemy in the Dark
♥

The sawdust on her kiss
Makes you crave the sweetness
You once found in my lips

Alchemy in the Dark

Mid air hanging frozen minutes
poised along the edges of whispers
like held breath dreading the exhale
pin drop silences warning growls
but a better conversation
than the murmured softness of goodbye
there is comfort here
miserable stability as we choose nothing
over the inevitability of farewell
the storm rages from my lungs to tongue
and the respiration of tears crack a reality
I no longer own
so I resist the urge to respire
head down, slow asphyxiation
if I do not yield...
if I hold time hostage in suffocated air
we go on forever.

Alchemy in the Dark
♥

Ribbon crisscrosses on your hands
each layer overlaid with pleas
binding hateful love
no more can I endure
satin barrier to prevent my reaching
stupidly forgiveness lingers
on my traitor tongue
shaking in this skin
withdrawal seeps through
resolve precariously balanced
too heavy for this ledge to hold
teeth grinding demonic symphony
The fall is costly
I know I shall break
lay shattered upon cold pavement
but at least I'll be whole in pieces
not slowly giving myself away
loving you contributes
to my own destruction

Alchemy in the Dark

Love in Dissection
drink the life from my marrow
rip apart to see what's inside
the pulse of you sustains
where did I go?
listless dreaming
drained the life from us
excise out the cancer
a shard here, a shard there
splintered wreckage love
No wonder I grew cold
piece it back together
knit the bones anew
construct from blueprints
paint by numbers perfection
this calculated passion
is how we lost our way
I wanted the wolves in your blood
you gave me watered down wine

I allowed attachments to people to define my worth. And of course, when things didn't work out, it reinforced that I wasn't good enough. Despite my best efforts to prove I was worth keeping around, people still left. I felt abandoned. Lost. Unlovable. I devoted so much of myself to others. Not realizing I could love myself.

Alchemy in the Dark

♥

it is said
the eyes are the windows to the soul
then what does it mean
when the image of you
is haunting shuttered lids?

Alchemy in the Dark

Something keeps pulling me back
run and run and run
never for too long
you touch me with words
and I sing along
I've lost myself in your stars
time and again
pulled into your gravity
gentle with this soul please
Lifted so high on wings
I've forgotten the ground
collision course with fate
my greatest story
or my worst fall
remains to be seen

Alchemy in the Dark
♥

Sometimes I fear your fantasy of me
is more intriguing than my reality...

Alchemy in the Dark

my heart is your heart
and all that dwells within
agony to know its secrets kept
the places that ache
for touch or whispered word
desires longing to scream
the madness burning there
that must be confined in silence
for if it is allowed a voice
the roaring would collapse the tower
all precariously held by fragile fear
terrifying unknown haunts my beloved
and I the ghost in your dreams
the apparition of love lost
of roads not taken
of all that was abandoned
to live a life safe in misery
for that was the easier path
reminding you what the price
of trepidation has cost.

Alchemy in the Dark

your soul screaming infiltrates
a feral plea my heart can hear
Visceral and raw
drowning under the weight
of your world crashing in
surrender my love
let it collapse all around
Find peace in the free fall
I'll be waiting
on the other side of destruction

Alchemy in the Dark

I don't know how to stop
looking for us
when dancing with strangers.

Alchemy in the Dark

Devastation imminent when dawn comes to call
the whispered goodbye on horizon's lips
as you slip through the cracks of dream and awake
only in those small hours of sleep
are you mine
whether fantasy or delusion... you are mine
only to be stolen again and again from me
every flip of the hourglass
time is a thief...
lost into mists of hazy consciousness
and here is morning in blushed complexion
heralded in by joyful sunrise
like it was supposed to make letting you go effortless
Like my heart didn't just shatter with the first breath of daybreak

Alchemy in the Dark

you were meant to just numb all the pain
whiskey and fire
just burn it all away
a temporary respite
a place to forget
I never intended to love you
I never wanted to fall again
and now here I am
haphazard leaping into stardust tipped hope
awaiting the most agonizingly beautiful death.

Alchemy in the Dark

I never wanted perfect. I wanted someone to see the beauty in my disaster.
To want to stay and grow with me. Twin souls climbing above our wounded spirits.
I needed someone to recognize my pain and not be afraid.

Alchemy in the Dark

I want the messy parts of you
the things you hide
all the ugliness found in the deep
all that screams to be heard
to be loved with the same ferocity
of that which shines
Let me see what hurts
the scars begging for air
I crave your humanity

Alchemy in the Dark

somewhere tonight
you're holding her hand
thinking about me
lost in memory
your thumb grazes hers
searching, almost pleading for a spark
Only cold and empty greet you
remembering the voltage between us
how your skin felt against mine
Does her kiss whisper my name
when you close your eyes?
You hold her tighter
praying you can forget
The perfection of us
How my curves fit the edges of you
and that she can't hear your heart
scream for me

Alchemy in the Dark

it is a terrible thing to love the fantasy of a person
and keep them dangling in the abyss of indecision.

Alchemy in the Dark

♥

maybe it was the haze of my abandonment issues
or the way I got so inebriated off your kiss
that somewhere between the sticky glow of bar lights
and the cool leather of your backseat
embracing my lonely skin
that I swapped sense for codependency
believing it was love

Alchemy in the Dark

Marrow uninhabited
withered roses dust neglected fantasy
Cheeks of hollowed shadow
now dry empty pools of salt
give me a soul just for a little while
stir my insides
Dry rot breathing relieved
Borrow the beating in your chest
mimic shadows dancing
rent my bones
until they remember how to be alive

Alchemy in the Dark

the moon my confessor
on her studded midnight throne
taking in the tears of my secrets
reigning above her glittering court
but no absolution will she grant me
no forgiveness of my sin to love you as I do
when I know you are as forbidden to me
as golden apples on innocent spring lips
stolen from ancient holy gardens
yet we both found ourselves bitten
suddenly knowing more
conspirators of carnal invocations
dabbling in the arcane knowledge of flesh and spirt
finding the balance of wicked desire and the uniting of souls
daring to breathe for only each other
and it is that transgression I am now branded
my punishment the eternal beat of your heart
haunting the blood in my veins.

Alchemy in the Dark

♥

Swallow him down without a care
a hopeful sedative on frayed veins
with a prayer I beseeched the stars
for deliverance from the remains of you
I felt him knocking on scarred doors
the places blistered desperately raw
feverishly trying to burn you away
but I could not be seen
shying away from anything deeper
dwelling in the shallow
for even in the most grotesque agony
I would rather suffer alone
than risk being another of the rejected
For who would want a disfigured heart?

Alchemy in the Dark
♥

for a few minutes
I was home
Only to watch your kiss
turn to driver's dust in my rear view

Alchemy in the Dark

there is never enough of time
elusive forever taunting loudly ticking minutes
never enough of the taste of us
mingled kisses stolen in rushed moments
never enough hours basking in afterglow
never enough of you

Alchemy in the Dark

You were everything to me...

Except mine.

Alchemy in the Dark
♥

he's not you...
when I breathe, I bite my tongue
Fearful of open mouth kisses
Will he see the love song written there
betrayal of secret truths burst forth
and your name is exhaled

Alchemy in the Dark
♥

Lamenting to the moon
Tear-stained remembrances fill the heavy night
a million falling stars and not one wish answered
where are you, beloved?
I pretend my prayers reach your dreams
and you feel me in the waves of moonlight
you're right here yet so far
Is my mind playing tricks
or do you hear me as I hear your voice calling from under water
Time has not dulled this ache
absence has not diminished this love
is it real or my curse
that the dark whispers a promise of hope

Alchemy in the Dark

midnight drives going nowhere
just me and the music
with only the glow of cigarettes
and your memory for company

Alchemy in the Dark
♥

You'll never get the taste of me
Out of your mouth
Forever cursed craving more.

Alchemy in the Dark
♥

why do we have to break so hard
   can't simply walk away from yesterdays
      haunted in "what if" and hovering "should have"
         The sticky trap of "had I only" shackles
           iron would have been lighter
            softer for brittle bones
              key swallowing magic acts hold no glamour
            only shedding light on time thieves
           prison bars of dusty sunlight
               Raise my lips like I'm catching snowflakes
             where was the sweetness I remember?
          The joy of innocent moments
       this domino road chased me here
     cascade effect feeding urgent fear of survival
      I let it keep crashing around me
      jumbled roads that never end
      self-sabotaging tunnel maze
           had I only seen the stair steps they made
          invisible ink writing on the wall
             pointing to overlooked doorways.
          that first broken breath
            guttural sobs breathing crushed glass
        perhaps the torment will cleanse me
      release my sins
     to some holy place
       that is as distant
             as the taste of your last kiss

Alchemy in the Dark
♥

doubtful as I am stained
by rogue evocations
of something so intertwined
permeating even the most remote shadows
I am lost amongst debris
the riptide carries me
to distant shores of unknown beasts
growling bloodthirsty to consume
the carcass of us
do I fight to save what remains?
allow the carnivorous jaws of pain
to devour until we are nothing
but sun-bleached ivory
vacantly staring into used to be?

Alchemy in the Dark

♥

she tastes of barbed wire cages
lulling cyanide sweetness
with belladonna eyes...
but I know you'll still keep her
even though she's slowly killing your soul.

Alchemy in the Dark

The tidal wave of me will consume you
my soul overindulging in you
I just want to forget me and firmly implant myself
into your heart and mind
the barbs of my contrived love bearing its own poison
as much as I want to prove I'm worth some small crumb
your rejection feeds the sickness in my shadow
corroborating the lies I sing to myself
that I'll never be worth loving.

Alchemy in the Dark

Mourning all that could never have been
but yet was the best of us
you haunt the forgotten places
those that ached so long
the pain etched there
interlaced in the cadence of my soul
grinding out your name
in the most bittersweet love requiem

Alchemy in the Dark
♥

Shivers in the winter chill
the cold welcome anesthetic
maybe if I sit here long enough
sip the icy air in shattered swallows
it will numb the parts of you
that still breathes in my bones

Alchemy in the Dark

I ache in the places
that used scream your name
with such intensity
that their echoes scarred the walls

Alchemy in the Dark

Today, I realized I've been holding my breath
believed all had been forgiven
been transcended beyond
all that had gone before...
then you spoke barbed truths
and while I am grateful you trusted me
with your haunted thoughts
I find an arrow unexpectedly
shattering into raw places I forgot existed

Alchemy in the Dark

I'm in an in-between state of knowing
I'm enough for myself
but realizing I'm not enough for you.

Alchemy in the Dark

you built your own cage
bars of fear and doubt
a soul silently screams
desperate to be free
you dare not breathe
not realizing how fragile
your captors are
if you only find the courage
to exhale and let it all fall down

Alchemy in the Dark

♥

Watered down shades of muted silence
you can't even recognize your own reflection
all to be someone else's version of perfect
I want to feed your soul
remind you of your wild
unshackled and free to shine
unearth the beauty in being yourself
For every atom of mine thinks
every atom of yours is absolute perfection.

Alchemy in the Dark

I told him he was beautiful
uncomfortable uncertainty smiled on his lips
and the doubt in his blush
broke my heart

Alchemy in the Dark
♥

You were all I could breathe
And now there's is no air
Inhaled fairytale fragments
burning in my lungs

Alchemy in the Dark

Empty fingers try to entice
your insides scream for mercy
while your skin pretends
the recoil is pleasure shivers
forced kisses regret
sending you reeling back to autumn nights
moonlight memories of me
a twisted medicine for the pain
smiling for me
reliving moments of kaleidoscopic rapture

Alchemy in the Dark
♥

she may have the mundane parts of you
      The guilty obligation you are driven to extend
            but you see me when you close your eyes

Alchemy in the Dark

your watch was an hour behind
our eyes never meeting on time
My perfume on a breeze
your heart longing
for what it couldn't remember
until the minutes sped up
finally we arrived
the pulse of you
felt in my bones
the joy of finding fate
marred by bitter regret
as her talons gripped your arm

Alchemy in the Dark

Did you dream of me?
Unbidden haunting your heart
Carved my place inside your ivory
I'm the shimmer you desire

Alchemy in the Dark

These dark words on my tongue
your kiss swallows
dirt into diamonds
bringing me back to the sun
the antidote against myself

Alchemy in the Dark

Haunting specters still cling to my skin
taunting my resolve
at war between want and need
I know I can't keep you

Alchemy in the Dark
♥

I am to be your magic
the source of all your madness
A longing in your bones
missing pieces you try to find
desperately hoping to recreate
a light softly burning
reminder of what was lost

Alchemy in the Dark
♥

I don't want to ask.
I don't want to beg.
I don't want to cry.
I want you to just know.
To be loved the way I love.

Alchemy in the Dark
♥

Often, it's not them you ache for.
 you grieve the pieces of yourself that got left behind.

Alchemy in the Dark

We are parallel horizons
Praying one day our stars converge

Alchemy in the Dark

it's in the quiet I miss you most
when my mind has a chance to wander
and my heart has a moment to remember

Alchemy in the Dark

It was by allowing myself to feel pain
that I could begin to transform.
By acknowledging the dark parts of myself, my wounds
around relationships, that I could let love touch me.

BEAUTIFUL SURRENDER

Alchemy in the Dark

Surrender

Love is the thing we all dream of whether we admit it or not. Great love stories play out on screens and in books and feed this insatiable fantasy. However, love isn't just a romantic fantasy. It's a power. Real, true unconditional love of the self and others can change lives. Yet it's the hardest thing to do. To choose love as this is sometimes making incredibly hard choices. But it's never wrong to love. This was me surrendering to all love means.

Alchemy in the Dark

We tried to run from each other
Forget all that crackled between us
But our souls starve
Without the alchemy our bones create

Alchemy in the Dark
♥

Regardless of how this goes
Or where it ends…
You were always worth the risk

Alchemy in the Dark
♥

I don't want to just love you.
I want our souls to merge and burn brighter
than any star found in the universe.

Alchemy in the Dark
♥

Stars called your name
irresistibly my voice compelled to sing harmony
I think it was the shine in your eyes
or his how your reckless spirit encouraged mine
we became a force
orbiting each other
exhilaration of the dance
twisting push and pull
Lifted beyond on the call of universe
Dizzying high as the ground disappeared below
Drunk on ecstasy I scarcely noticed the world change
numbing the rip of my skin when you stole my heart

Alchemy in the Dark
♥

                                        she lit your world up
soul concocted of fireworks and gasoline
                          dangerous and unexpected

Alchemy in the Dark

Vulnerable heart trying to stay hidden
shield all that lay raw under my skin
but you had a power
Something in me spellbound
Terrifying yet intriguing
a way of knowing me without words
and my shaking soul
begged to be naked with you.

Alchemy in the Dark
♥

The way you reached me is indescribable. I had sturdy walls that had remained impenetrable for a lifetime. You didn't demand or storm them. You didn't take my fortress by storm. It was gentle. Subtle. A slow dance under the stars. You seduced all of me, even the parts that were terrified. I found myself letting you in without realizing. This overwhelming desire to connect with you flooded my soul.

Alchemy in the Dark

♥

All I can promise you is adventures, laughter and wild love.
The rest will unfold as it's meant to.

Alchemy in the Dark

she was the type that burned from the inside out
a magnetic pull not to be denied
a raging wildfire hell bent on destruction
but it wasn't to hurt to you
her soul will wake you up
with a breathless kiss that leaves you transmuted
forever changed, her love frees your heart
resplendent is she, lighting up your shadows
fought your demons until even they knelt at her feet
she will heal even the most twisted of your scars
if you are brave enough to invite her in.

Alchemy in the Dark
♥

After years of losing who I was,
it was within you that I found myself.
Finally, my bones felt right in my skin.
You gave me a place to be vulnerable.
Naked and laid bare.
There was no more hiding. You saw me.
It was with you that I discovered what forgiveness was.
What healing felt like.
To be loved without labels or conditions.
No expectations to limit the expanse of our dreams.
It was with you that I found the in-between. The wild yet safe.
Savage but tender. Maddening passion rooted deep
to keep me from drifting too far.
The coalescing of love into lust.
I knew before our skin touched.
Before our lips sparked and all hell broke loose.
We created something alchemical.
We had stars in our veins.
You and I touched souls.

Alchemy in the Dark
♥

you are everything
I never dreamed could be possible.
The most beautifully terrifying thing in the world.
The thing that transforms souls.
Love.
and now there's no way of ever going back.

Alchemy in the Dark

Through golden stars
Or the piercing underbrush
We have crawled back
Not just to each other
But to ourselves.

Alchemy in the Dark
♥

if I lingered too long at your lips
tarried fingers reluctant to release
the pulse connecting us
it's only to keep the absence of you at bay
just a few moments longer

Alchemy in the Dark

♥

somewhere there's a southern breeze
that still blushes as it whispers our names
through the places that even now burn with our memories
places kissed by the wildfire that raged between us

Alchemy in the Dark
♥

                if I could bottle you up
               I'd drink of you everyday
                    as you are the most
                seductive intoxication
that I've ever surrendered to

Alchemy in the Dark
♥

push pull push pull
magnets flipping quarters
to see who's going to run this time
knowing all the while
the road leads right back
to each other

Alchemy in the Dark

We are a collision course to nowhere
that is everything desired
so much myself with you
my soul aches
take me down with you
I promise to make beauty of the shadows
hold you through the unknown
find adventure in uncertainty
knowing I'd rather fall with you in the dark
than see the stars with anyone else.

Alchemy in the Dark
♥

the sun did not touch your face
overshadowed by far more insidious beasts
watching the way they creeped and crawled
stealing the light from your eyes
I wanted nothing more than kiss you in that moment
let my warmth remind
something tangible to reveal you are loved
loosen your tongue with mine
banish the monsters that plagued you into silence
allow the words unsaid
to spill into me
and I could make them beautiful again
hands caressing cheeks
hold you tight and breath into you
that you are most precious
some cherished treasure
even when your smile is lost

Alchemy in the Dark

Loving you was like coming home. It felt safe to be myself. No masks, no hiding. With you I had a place to explore who I was. A place without judgment or fear. The only rejection I felt was created in my own mind. I began to dismantle my wounds. See how I was hurting myself more than anyone else ever could.

Alchemy in the Dark

as much as we were lust
unbridled lovers pouring out as shaken champagne
there was a natural duality
where there was impassioned chaos
there was the comfort of safety
where there was deception
there was truth
you were all that inflamed me
and yet I've never felt more safe

Alchemy in the Dark

my love will survive the taste of death
when all withers into aged parchment promises
vows once impassioned vibrating vocal cords
now mere memories on the whispered winds
yet we will not fade
we will not succumb to nothingness
or linger along photographic edges
like we only existed in faded stories
No...
you will never be gone from me
my soul is stained, marked, branded in your existence
and should they read my bones like tea leaves
they will find you embedded in the dust of my blood

Alchemy in the Dark

you're a faded photograph
in the pocket of my favorite faded jeans
all the pain and love embedded in film
held close until we leap from paper kisses
a reminder of hope
or maybe of foolishness
as I wait for you to come home.

Alchemy in the Dark

I am wracked with need.
The need to be seen.
The need to be heard.
the need to be wanted beyond all doubt.
The need to be touched with certainty.
The need to be held with such passion.
the need for someone who will not hesitate to rip me open and love all that's inside.

Alchemy in the Dark

awakened the hidden in me
you were the only one
who has ever ran their fingers
down the spine of my soul
left me quivering with a craving of more...
that's why I stayed here in the dark so long
aching to detonate into falling stars.

Alchemy in the Dark

It was every soft sunrise
the ombre beauty of twilight
shyness of stars on the blackest midnight
the mysterious depths of oceans
the beauty and the danger lurking in hidden currents
undeniable pull of lightning seeking
the safety of the earth
something to ground the chaos
we were all that was good in the world
and all that was wrong
we were everything to each other.

Alchemy in the Dark

♥

gasoline fumes over open flames
trip wire lips aching to detonate
to bring the rush of fire
into dead behind the eyes way of being
we came alive together
we would never be the same
forever forged in glittered steel
to say we were explosive in love
would be an understatement.

Alchemy in the Dark

I know you believe yourself to be under my spell
that I possess some charm, some magic
spiderweb silks spun delicately around your heart
but it is I that is bewitched
unable to be free of the memory
your kiss burned into my lips
the scarred mark of your love
branding my soul as yours
an incurable affliction
that is both pleasure and pain
maddening insanity to love you as I do
where my mind no longer feels my own
leaving an unbearable restlessness
when you are gone from me too long

Alchemy in the Dark

Wild horses thunder in your blood
Reach out to brush their beauty
Soft fingers linger only a moment
Fear doubts your eyes
As you feel me inside
We collide in the chase
Shy away from all that is
Fight the beckoning unknown
The savage stallion begging
I'd never try to reign you in
Only love you across the divide
Run free. Baby
Until your heart calls you back.

Alchemy in the Dark

She holds onto the faith
That someone somewhere one day
Will not only love her as wild as she is
But be inspired by the adventure in her soul

Alchemy in the Dark

We were two ordinary people
With extraordinary love
Oh, how jealous the stars!
Graceful in falling tribute
To how we made the night shimmer.

Alchemy in the Dark

♡

my breath gets caught in the stumbles my heart makes whenever you look at me.

Alchemy in the Dark
♥

we bend but never break
tempest tested and rise
come together only to drift once more
we run, we chase
love until it's too much
retreat into silence
we become stagnant bodies with screaming souls
then when the absence is deafening
we find each other again

Alchemy in the Dark
♥

She was the type of girl
Who preferred the simplicity of country nights,
the magic of fireflies,
the singing of bullfrogs,
and the beauty of the moon.

Alchemy in the Dark
♥

she dreamed not only of passion filled nights
pinned under savage kisses and hungry hands
staying awake until dawn caught the moaning night
but the simplicity of sunlit laughter
spontaneous dancing under kitchen lights
of fingers interlaced on drives going nowhere
silent smiles from across crowded rooms
she dreamed of being with someone
who had the courage to love her loudly.

Alchemy in the Dark

I need you inside me.
Not just my body though.
I need you in my mind.
I need you in my heart.
I need you in my soul.
Invade me, ravage me, love me
and set me on fire.
Make me come alive again.

Alchemy in the Dark

I have faith in what will come
but some part of me fears I'll suffocate
from holding my breath.

Alchemy in the Dark

I clung to your love too tightly at times. My life raft in a sea of doubt and not yet healed abandonment. You taught me to let go. That sometimes space and distance aren't villains but necessary ebbs and flows designed to make us look inward. To find within ourselves what we expect others to give.

Alchemy in the Dark

I want the forever of sunrises with you
the nightly expanse of your sunsets
the in-between of breathing your days
and watching stars call your name

Alchemy in the Dark
♥

Animalistic nights moaning at the moon.
Bruised lips and marked skin.
Then in the morning, sweet kisses on my
forehead as dawn peeks through the window.
All while we lay tangled up in laughter and each other
The sweet with the obscene are the wishes I hold dear

Alchemy in the Dark

She is everything that terrifies him.
She is the unknown.
All soul and Magic.

Alchemy in the Dark

You were everything.
my love.
my pain.
My mirror.
And all of my madness

Alchemy in the Dark

Her soul trusted him.
her heart loved him.
her body wanted him.
That made him dangerous.

Alchemy in the Dark
♥

unbidden your kiss enters my prayers
unholy images turn my thoughts
to the moonlight glinting off your skin
I call out but
it is your name I breathe
the burn from your lips
is larceny of my heart
surely I have sold my soul
and I'm not sure I care.

Alchemy in the Dark
♥

How I craved the sun on our kiss
instead of broken moonlight shadows
writing the secrets on our lips.

Alchemy in the Dark
♥

It's not just your bare skin I desire
I want your heart quivering naked
spread apart before me
shivering as I taste the secrets
Buried within

Alchemy in the Dark
♥

My old self sat silent in the sheds of a snakeskin
No less beautiful just a home now too small
For the growth in my soul

Alchemy in the Dark

I want someone who is inspired by my whimsy.
Finds the magic in leaf piles
and the beauty of kissing under thundering skies.
A person who would never let me dance in the rain alone

Alchemy in the Dark

♥

Somewhere in a corner that aches
is the place where our love should have been.
In the absence of myself
I found you
expecting the nothingness as is typical
filling all the void with self-sacrifice
paper doll in motion
somewhere in the midst of losing myself
the compass of your hands guided
laying souls bare
Gently demanding I reclaim all that was lost
there was safety in your smile
your eyes full of my reflection
letting me see myself whole

Alchemy in the Dark
♥

> I never saw stars in his eyes
> the sing song lilt of a fairytale
> but my demons met his shadow's gaze
> and instantly fell crazy in love

Alchemy in the Dark

It was never that we weren't enough
We were too much
Too intense
Too tangled
Too wild
Too mirrored
It wasn't only that we loved
It was something devastatingly more.

Alchemy in the Dark

you will never fade
or wither for me
forever immortal
in my mind and memory

Alchemy in the Dark

♥

Let's rewrite this story
all that kept us apart
disappearing into lover's dust
dismantling the past
searching inside Destiny's clouded head
for reason, for hope
an explanation for the cruelty
the theft of unlived memories
living unfulfilled
a void unsatisfied
forge ahead and find ourselves there
convergent roads
on skeletal remains of time
change our fallen stars
so they collide

Alchemy in the Dark

I scare you...
throat gulping, life shattering, chaos wielding force
that your whole being thirsts for
try to recreate
summon me like the devil on your shoulder
strain to hear my voice in her words
will your pulse to quicken
in otherworldly explosions
but met with disappointing mediocre lip service
to the alchemy of me
suffered silence wistful thwarted desire
craving a soul storm to descend
like only I can

Alchemy in the Dark

Ensnared between shaking fingers
butterfly wings
 in tickled breezes upon my palms
intricate fragility
My heart bloomed in your beauty
desperation looms over cloudy skies
as I fear loosening my grip
shall make a path for escape
velvet soft you nestle
cupped lovingly inside me
I hope the weight in these hands
doesn't crush the spirit within

Alchemy in the Dark
♥

She brought the magic back into your life.
That little bit of stardust
reminding you of all that could be.

Alchemy in the Dark

we are unbreakable
no matter the distance
reticent words falling in waves
immortally mine
fated red ribbons bind
close those eyes
and breathe exhale until you find me
together dancing in the veil
the safety of dreams
bring me home, my love
taste me, feel me
hear my heart speaking what my voice cannot
in here we can simply be
love however we wish
laying amongst whispering stars

Alchemy in the Dark

♥

>instant recognition
>my soul knew you
>before our lips ever touched

Alchemy in the Dark

it's easy to catch my body
hold the curves
and make it roar
but rare a soul
that captures my heart
feel the beat
peer within the shadows
unlock the depths of secrets
and my dearest love...
you have done both

Alchemy in the Dark
♥

my mark is etched into your soul
there will always be a beat in your heart that belongs to me

Alchemy in the Dark
♥

you are all my original sin
the fires of passion and fine lines walking
all the wrongs that feel soul shattering right
the compass to the depth of me
my true North
stars that alight when my feet find the way
all my roads to redemption

Alchemy in the Dark
♥

You turn me like no one ever has. It's this mix of pure love and pure lust for you that just hit
 everything just right and it's absolutely intoxicating, addicting and makes me insatiable for
you....

Alchemy in the Dark

Our love was like sand seduced by waves.
 Sometimes it was the lazy, gentle caress of star struck lovers.
Lost in foamy lace and blushing sunlight.
Other times, the violent collision
 of ravenous paramours trying to consume each other.
Storm driven frenzy crashing relentlessly
 until passion is finally spent.

IGNITE MY WILD

Alchemy in the Dark

Ignite

Some view lust as something dirty. For me lust and passion are one in the same. It's desire. It's life itself. You can have a lust for many things. Sexual lust is a healing energy. It's a connection of mind, body and soul. It certainly is true for me. I lived without it for a long time. I felt robotic and lost the beauty of what life should be. Rediscovering this part of myself was key in my journey.

Alchemy in the Dark

Honey dipped lust starved
maddening the taste of you
glide along forbidden terrain
the arch of my back until heaven shatters
cradle me until I fall from bliss
then slowly put the pieces back
one by one with salacious tongue
draw out the secrets
written in sugar on my thighs
until my lips scream your name
and call down the stars

Alchemy in the Dark

my name clinging to your lips
embedded barbs into soft skin
 seductive hex lounging
darkly upon your shoulder
reminded in every kiss
how you crave my taste
close your eyes with futile wishes
your fingers will feel my curves taunting
remembering firework undulations
a scorn of bitter regret taints
gaze longingly my darling love
 into shades of blues and grays
only the reflection of me shall whisper
faint imitations driving to madness
satisfaction elusive in her teasing
never grace your body to release

Alchemy in the Dark
♥

a thousand moments
spent in tangled sheets
redolent of us
a thousand more
dying breathless in your arms
vehement arching ecstatic death
brought back time and again
by the ravenous ache
for your hands on my body

Alchemy in the Dark

when I can't find the words,
let my body sing you a love song

Alchemy in the Dark

ignite me
I've been asleep far too long
I need the ferocious pull of you
the untamed in you waking this wild woman
a feral kiss takes me to the edge
Gasping inhaling you
set aflame and let me burn to ash
stroke my cinders until I catch the heat
immortal embers a soft glow
embracing that dark is where home is
where I shine the brightest
and in your arms we are twisting firestorms
the violent way we come together
the most beautiful disaster
tempests in chaos
fall and rise never do we waver
light up the night with me, beloved
we make each other alive.

Alchemy in the Dark

And there we stood
surrounded in night sky
we were Gods
divinity in the cascading beat
of your heart against mine
time could not catch us
heaven's breath held still
and our lips threw such sparks
it put the stars to shame

Alchemy in the Dark

                    I'm under your skin
                   like a prayer or a curse
                  you love the wickedness
                    I lace in your blood

Alchemy in the Dark

Wander the wilderness of your soul
seek out the hidden wonders there
exquisite creatures in the dark expanse
I would love even the wildest of you first
before I ravage across the passion
trembling in your body
taste the chaos there
teasing fingers drawing breath
get lost in the waves
and not care if I ever find my way back.

Alchemy in the Dark
♥

I have a madness for the way you look at me
an insatiability for the soft yet savage lust in your lips
the delicious burn
bordering upon obsession

Alchemy in the Dark

Pinned to the wall, he kissed me breathless. held my chin between strong fingers, whispering, "You should be kissed like that everyday." And for the first time since you walked away, I felt hope. That perhaps I was something special. A tiny glimmer that someone wanted what you threw away.

Alchemy in the Dark
♥

I want to feed on you like a woman starved

        consume you until you only remember my name

                overfilled ecstatic contortions
your body bends for me
beckons flirtatious lips to commit
the most outrageous sins upon your flesh
swallow the adrenaline throbbing need
eyes locking my tease to your fervent desire
brimming with promises yet kept
that you may be delivered from evil seductions
my throat purring when you become feral under my spell
boundary pushed and delectable raw rapture exposed
until your hand captures this wild creature
run your tongue up my soul
and savagely love me.

Alchemy in the Dark
♥

come play with me in the moonlight
littered with dead stars and makeshift memories
they shiver through the trees
much like my spine against your fingers
this pretend world the last shred of us
that we have to cling to
the carnal whispering of our darkest secrets
no longer contained breaking free of locked dams
we spark in defiance
all the dark bearing witness to the eclipsed love
 echoing between us
as the eyes in the night watch our souls collide.

Alchemy in the Dark

No matter where you go
what you do
how many lips you kiss
how many women fall prey to your eyes
somewhere deep inside
there will be a thirst you cannot quench
a wild insatiable hunger that gnaws at your mind
a burning ache driving you to madness
and there I'll be
stained evocations of me taunting
teasing whispers you can't quite touch
an affliction you can never let go of
as I am the magic in your bones

Alchemy in the Dark

feel that...
   right there...
the crackle of electricity
the palpable beat humming between us
the call of your body to mine
it's heat, it's tension
passion burning at both ends
of catastrophic dynamite
we could lose it all
or descend into new beginnings
vexed souls raging
against even the slightest distance
 all we crave is to be inside each other
skin to skin
soul to soul
a tangle of moans
weaving alchemical echoes
knowing once we do...
we will never be the same

Turn to me love
expose all that dwells inside
I have a lustful curiosity
to know your soul.

Alchemy in the Dark

let my fingers marvel at the perfection of you
until even the night whimpers for liberation
I want to release the stars from your bones

Alchemy in the Dark
♥

The deliciously sadistic way you talk to me
makes even the devil in me blush

Alchemy in the Dark

Lust was our original connection. We blindly entered into it without thought of what may come. It took almost losing you to make me see this was something more. Something bigger than we'd ever imagined. The openness of our desires built an unshakable foundation for love.

Alchemy in the Dark

possession, obsession robbed of myself
elaborate playground for your imagination

Alchemy in the Dark
♥

Shaking hands on hotel doorknobs. I could scarcely breathe. Open doors, descending storm of passion and urgency. We didn't talk. At least not with words, but oh did our bodies sing. There was a moment when the doorway intimately got to know my spine. Your hand on my throat and your tongue in my mouth... your other hand seeking the long-neglected conjunction of my thighs... the delectable collision of lips...

You kissed me like were starving for me. Not just my skin but you were hungry for my soul. We swallowed each other whole, a fierceness, an intensity I'd never felt from you. You pulled away slowly to look at me. We were left breathless, insatiable. Bruised lips and wet thighs thundered in protest. I couldn't bear even the smallest of distances between us. I needed you. All of you. We transform together. Something out of reach with anyone else. I needed us.

Alchemy in the Dark

♥

we keep flirting with lines that shouldn't be crossed.
And the way you make my body ache...
makes my mind not give damn.

Alchemy in the Dark
♥

I dare you...
let go, my love
meet me on plains of silver stars
where midnight goes on forever
dripping slow aching carnality
I dare you...
Abandon all that binds
replacing heaviness of chains
with satin ribbon embraces
words making love to skin
I dare you...
Come to me arms outstretched
graze the valleys of your hips
 lip skimming seduction
sweat gilded glow intoxication
I dare you...
Fall for something new
the intricate tangles offering up a wilderness
unearth the feral in your soul
risk it all to sip the blood of mine
I dare you...

Alchemy in the Dark
♥

I miss whispering sheet choirs praising heavens
while we danced between them
and how they blushed when I screamed your name.

Alchemy in the Dark

The lust we have for each other set us free. Free from cages forcing us to be what others wanted us to be. Lust let us be raw. Not just open bodies seeking pleasure but souls bursting to delve into curious creativity. We found ourselves in sexual expression. We found an unwillingness to settle for mundane or mediocre. Lust was a battle cry in the fight for ourselves.

Alchemy in the Dark

you've painted me a night's sky
    sewn in all the best parts
        diamond encrusted moon beams
            make us drunk and prone to follies
            of lovers getting lost in warm breezes
                on the wildflower bed
            we find our way down winding paths
                  and carnal seascapes
              oh, the adventures your lips
                found on my skin
              let's get our hands dirty
              build our castles
          be it brick, branch
         or beautiful delusion
        fashion me a crown of stars
     with honey dripping
    soothe the ache that dares to grumble
premonition of the shattered love
      I'd willingly fall on the blade for
          lay spent amongst the long grass ramparts
              diverting the rising sun
                  spinning possibilities
            like we had the most magnificent plan

Alchemy in the Dark

your mouth reveres your queen
      again and again
           until dawn forces my abdication
             cascade over me in relentless waves
              until my breath is caught
            impel into me feed this body until I shatter
              violent gluttony I want all of you
         splinter into intoxicated divinity
      sheathed in velvet rapture
    graceful falling upon sweat slicked satin
a willing victim of salacious love

Alchemy in the Dark

♥

my Eden
I dare to trespass across your skin
dare to delight in this brazen divinity
the heavens in starlight on your lips
flows into my parched veins
kindled sparks inflame
twist my insides
elicit all I've been forbidden to dream
when with you all seems possible
all seems within hungry grasp
worshipped moans unfettered
clenched fingers entrapped in cotton bonds
this is my church
where my prayer is ridden on twisted hips
it's a body unleashed as my soul sings for you
you capture me heat trembled
voracious need for us to crash all over again

Alchemy in the Dark

♥

oh, the way we sparkle
summer asphalt shimmer kind of heat
dancing between us
waltzing across the shivered beat
of passion stormed lips
a magic only summoned
when my lace collides with your skin

Alchemy in the Dark
♥

my imagination knew the taste of you
long before my lips ever graced your skin

Alchemy in the Dark

♥

Soft lips open music box
grinding melody of skin and sweat
swallow ardent voices
whiskey warm and electric charged
the adrenaline I crave pounds in my veins
I'm high, I'm drunk on the look in your eyes
like you've kissed the sun
and soul abandoned in trembling corners
follow me down...
trail blazed in fire gasps
siren song luring you
into what we shouldn't do
but rush to commit
your lace gilded goddess
with bewitching tongue
writing triumph upon your skin
impelled to the edge dancing
where my name
is the only prayer your voice remembers
spiral riding until nothing else remains
theft of senses beyond pleasure shock
succumb, my darling
get lost in me

Alchemy in the Dark
♥

Kiss me slow
Repressed ecstatic longing
Erupting on swollen promises
Eternal lovers tongue tinged in secrets
Deeper still
Do not stop
Insistent questing pleasures arching
Spiral around the stars with me
Like you're trying to reach my soul

Alchemy in the Dark

I fight your gravity when I'm near you
aware of every breath you expel
every visible flicker of your heartbeat
 that pounds through thirsting veins
it's some siren song pulling me
a pulsating rhythm penetrating my core
a dance of devils calling my name
closer and closer still until we are mere gasps away
I imagine your kiss
a burning brand marking me yours
so any other's lips would taste sour
in comparison to the sweetness I find on yours
ruinous to love you as I do
but it matters not
as I'd rather succumb to this, to you
to this insanity of us
to never feel more alive
than when I'm with you

Alchemy in the Dark

In the emptiness of her fingers
You call out for me
You reached into her
To only come up empty
Your skin screams for mercy
Regret flooding pretend kisses
Sending you reeling back to April mornings
Hazy dawn drenched images of me
Smiling in the in-between
Reliving moments of kaleidoscopic pleasure

Alchemy in the Dark

Sometimes we are afraid to live with passion. Fear and doubt tie us to a life we settled for and are terrified of losing. Mediocre is safe. It's reliable. We crave stability and even though we may be miserable and unhappy, at least we know the outcome. That's not living. That is existing. It's survival. I want to do more than just survive.

Alchemy in the Dark

Come hither stares in crowded rooms
Painfully pretending you don't know
The curve of my lips
subtle teases build tension
Desire blazing in your gaze
A smirk in the dark
Pleading eyes begging for a taste
Knowing all you can think of
Is finding the space of pleasure
Where thigh meets lace

Alchemy in the Dark

Unbutton me a little more
With lips and fingers expose my soul
Interpret bursting sighs against relentless tongue
I've been unknowingly asleep
Unleash this wild buried inside
Waiting to be claimed

Alchemy in the Dark

Soul naked shivers
Words caress in spine curving syllabic symphony
Dusted blush of the unknown
Lifted lips achingly anticipating
Drawing out bleeding breath
Raw inside from feeling too much
Golden larynx vibrato pulls me from slumber
The grace in your hands melts stone
Midas touch makes me shimmer
This granite monster
Now your gilded goddess

Alchemy in the Dark
♥

I miss the storm you conjure in my body
the raging waves that bring such ecstasy
that I could detonate at just a look
the sight of you stirs a volcanic heat
rising, climbing to an insatiable burn
that I am again and again reborn
the build, the tension...
waiting to be devoured
clinging to the insanity you instill in my bones
oh, how I miss the taste of your chaos

Alchemy in the Dark
♥

hold still my love...
not just yet...
I know you've been waiting
wildly clawing the edges of pleasure
denied and pulled back
riding a quivering ache
my administrations slow... brutally deliberate
I enjoy watching you in agonizing hunger
pleading eyes and begging skin
wicked thoughts have plagued my mind
of arching hips and moaning breath
the taste of you leaving me drunk
I need to unburden my soul
confide the most salacious desires
to the harmony of your impatient whispers
I fear we may be here awhile...
my lips have many sins they want to confess

Alchemy in the Dark
♥

My soul isn't the only thing
   that wants to be naked with you

Thank you for reading my thoughts. I wish you courage in your dark times, the fierce joy of love and the playful deliciousness of your wild.

Have the adventure of your life.

-Lola Lawrence

ABOUT THE AUTHOR

Lola Lawrence lives in the small rural town of Arcanum, Ohio. She found a love of writing as a teenager and took several classes as her electives during her undergraduate degree. Lola has a B.S. in Behavioural-Social Sciences from Indiana University-East.

Lola is also a mother of three sassy, beautiful children with special needs. She is also a life coach. Her focus is on helping clients transform their lives, relationships, and achieve their dreams. She has been published in multiple anthologies for both poetry and short stories.

Lola enjoys photography, playing in her flower beds, reading and playing with her children.

This is her debut solo book.

Find Lola on:
Facebook: @Stirring The Soul
Instagram: @lolalawrence0507
Tik Tok: @lolalawrence0507
Twitter: @loladollkisses

Printed in Great Britain
by Amazon